Unlocking peak performa

Unlocking Peak Performance

Christie Kennard

Gower

© 1996 National Press Publications, Inc.
A Division of Rockhurst College Continuing Education
Center, Inc.

First published in the USA by National Press
Publications, Inc. as *Peak Performance*
This edition published by
Gower Publishing Limited
Gower House
Croft Road
Aldershot
Hampshire GU11 3HR
England

British Library Cataloguing in Publication Data
Kennard, Christie
    Unlocking peak performance
    1. Employee motivation 2. Incentives in industry
    I. Title
    658.3 '14

ISBN 0 566 07828 7

Printed in Great Britain by Biddles Ltd, Guildford

Contents

1

Motivation as a management tool

As an overworked manager you may feel that motivating your employees is not your problem. Ensuring your department's productivity is your job – meeting bottom-line quotas, not all this nonsense about recognition and team building. Staying motivated is up to your employees. After all, they possess some of the greatest motivators around: a regular pay cheque, job security and company benefits. But everybody needs to be motivated, from the Prime Minister down.

In this chapter we'll look at the difference

between 'job satisfiers' and what genuinely motivates employees to do their best.

Job satisfiers versus motivators

A university study revealed a dynamic value shift in the workforce that has created a motivation gap – the difference between what managers think their employees want and what employees actually want.

Employees were given a list of ten job factors and asked to rank them in importance from 1 to 10. Managers and supervisors were given the same list and asked to rank them the way they thought their employees would. The results were very illuminating. The managers and supervisors were often completely wrong about what really mattered most to their employees.

In the past, management considered employees' needs to be met by the traditional trio: pay rises, promotions and job security. Now all that is changing. Eighty per cent of today's workforce values more 'inner-directed' job motivators.

Money and perks are effective in the recruiting stage of attracting top candidates to a company, but they do not work as long-term motivators. Salaries, benefits, promotions, working conditions and company policies are basically job satisfiers – they keep workers satisfied with their jobs but they don't inspire them to go the extra mile.

Employees are motivated by having their basic

needs met, not just for survival but also for social and spiritual growth. Today's workers also are interested in work as a means of self-fulfilment. According to the study, what employees really want from their jobs is:

1. to be treated with respect;

2. an opportunity for personal growth;

3. self-expression in work and in life;

4. allowance for individual preferences and needs;

5. to be in a positive work environment which values employees as individuals;

6. information about their company's decisions and policies.

Maslow's hierarchy of needs

These needs closely parallel the hierarchy of needs defined by psychologist Abraham Maslow in *Motivation and Personality*. Maslow argued that people are motivated by different levels of needs and that lower-level needs must be met before higher-level needs. Maslow's hierarchy identified five levels of needs, listed in order below:

1. *Basic biological or physical needs.* These needs

include hunger, thirst and sleep. The work-place isn't where such needs are directly met. However, a pay cheque is the symbolic way in which employees assure themselves of food and shelter.

2. *Need for safety and security.* Employees can find a commitment to safety and security when their work environment incorporates fair play, job tenure, job protection and insurance.

3. *Belonging and social activity.* Man is a social creature. It's part of his social development to find satisfaction in belonging to and being accepted by a group. Often, that group consists of co-workers. Rather than discouraging subordinates from 'socializing' at work, managers can capitalize on this need by utilizing it to build strong teams.

4. *Enjoying esteem and status.* The desire for status, recognition, respect and acknowledgement of accomplishment are strong needs for many employees. Once they have acquired a certain expertise and made a significant contribution, they need to be rewarded. Smart managers initiate ways to recognize employees' contributions.

5. *Self-realization and fulfilment.* This last set of needs is the most likely to be overlooked by both employees and managers. People

often defer the pursuit of self-fulfilment because they are too busy satisfying social or status needs. Good managers understand their employees and know what it will take to help them achieve personal fulfilment.

Motivating by fulfiling needs

In the old days, bosses could use fear and coercion as motivators. The boss yelled and the work got done. There was always the threat – either explicitly stated or silently implied – of the employee's job hanging in the balance.

Today's managers realize that effective motivation is no longer simply a matter of dangling a carrot on a stick before their workers – providing financial rewards and penalizing failure. They achieve the greatest success by:

1. making sure basic needs are met (pay, benefits, job security);

2. creating a work climate where employees are given opportunities to fulfil their higher-level needs (social, esteem, self-fulfilment) and, therefore, willingly and enthusiastically work their hardest.

What do employees want?

No matter how mundane or repetitious their jobs, employees want them to be challenging; they want to derive personal meaning from their work. They need to know they're using their abilities to do a good job at something that is genuinely important.

Take a look at the people you manage and ask yourself if their jobs incorporate the following criteria for satisfaction:

1.   The job isn't monotonous to workers. They can change the pace by varying their tasks.

2.   The job doesn't waste employees' time and effort. Management has planned work in such a way that energy isn't exerted uselessly.

3.   Workers feel free to plan their own work and the ways they can do it most effectively.

4.   Workers feel they have a reasonable degree of authority and autonomy over how their work is done.

5.   Workers can correct their own errors and improve their own techniques.

6.   Workers don't feel too closely supervised, over-instructed or rigidly controlled by management.

7.   Workers see their work as an integral part of the whole company. Each worker is valued

as an individual, not seen as a cog in the machine.

8. Feedback from supervisors isn't embarrassing to workers. If it's praise, it's made public. If it's criticism, it's given in private.

People-friendly policies

According to Korn/Ferry International, an executive search firm, the workaholic syndrome that put top performers out in front a decade ago is fading away. More workers today are looking for companies that are 'family friendly'. This means offering a flexible work schedule so employees can share in important family events, secure decent care for dependents (elderly family members and children) and lead more fulfilled lives outside the workplace. To be effective, today's managers have to understand how to implement these changes. To be competitive, today's companies have to offer employees a range of work options unheard of in the past.

Whether or not your company's policies reflect the concerns of its employees, you as a manager should be sensitive to your staff's needs in balancing their home and work lives. By demonstrating your acceptance of the fact that the personal lives of your staff don't disappear at the office door, you'll be a more effective manager and better motivator. Here are five ways you can implement new policies and facilitate existing ones:

1. *Determine your employees' personal needs.*Don't assume you already know their needs. Do a needs assessment. Ask:

    ● how many of your employees are parents with child care needs?;

    ● how many are responsible for elderly parents?;

    ● what could you or the company be doing to help employees with family concerns?

2. *Look at time in a new way.* Consider initiating:

    ● flexi-time – consider a new look at scheduling, for instance allowing employees to arrive as early as 7 a.m. and stay until 6 p.m.; but once set, the schedule needs to be regular;

    ● job sharing;

    ● working at home – allowing employees to work at home often produces the same or better results than rigid work schedules.

3. *Make policies that match reality.* When working parents need to stay at home with sick children, they often use sick leave. If it's strictly defined to include only the time an employee is sick, it encourages dishonesty. Give

employees personal time that they can use to take care of personal business matters or sick relatives.

4. *Get the backing of other managers.* If your company resists change, get other departmental managers to support your approach.

5. *When employees make special requests, listen.* If employees propose a change such as working at home or job sharing, it may require the approval of unions, CEOs, sales managers, district managers, etc. Give your employee support to prove that an unusual work arrangement can succeed.

If you feel overwhelmed, you're not alone. You're part of the family now – an ever-extending network of relationships made up of companies, workers, their families, their friends and managers at work.

Summary

Above all, employees must feel they're working for a company that cares about them and their needs. They need to feel they're partners in making the business work.

You may think that communicating this to your employees is a lot of work. It is, but it comes with a payoff. Employees who feel their company needs them, cares about them and shares important information with them are your most valuable asset. Motivated employees can turn a sliding profit margin around, advertise your company, and keep you and your staff motivated and on track. Your job is to let it happen.

In the following chapters we'll look at ways to improve motivation – what works and what doesn't – through team building, communication, delegation and financial incentives. You can also assess how motivated you are and whether your company is doing all it can to ensure that its employees are happy, well compensated and free to do the best job possible.

2

Are you a motivated manager?

You've done everything possible to encourage your staff – from weekly pep talks to one-on-one meetings. Yet nothing seems to work. When you push for higher productivity, they tackle their jobs with all the enthusiasm of chain-gang workers. When you try the opposite tactic and lessen the pressure, they spend all their time chatting, indulging in extra-long lunches and personal phone calls.

What's wrong? Why aren't you able to motivate your staff more effectively?

The problem may be you. If you're not a motivated leader, your employees are the first to know. In this chapter we'll determine how motivated you really are. We'll take a look at:

- what motivation consists of and what the difference is between external and internal motivators;

- how you can improve your self-esteem;

- how your personal mission statement matches your company's;

- the characteristics of a motivated manager.

What is motivation?

It's difficult to motivate others unless you're already motivated. Are you motivated to do the best job you can? Are you enthused about going to your job each day? When employees, managers and owners are excited about their work, outstanding performance will follow.

Motivation and self-esteem are closely interrelated. Motivated employees feel good about themselves. People with high self-esteem naturally do a better job.

How motivated are you?

Do you consider yourself highly motivated, or is

your enthusiasm beginning to slip? Do you know how to protect and bolster your self-esteem or do you become easily upset and defensive when your work is being criticized?

To determine your level of motivation answer the following questions:

1. How long have you held your present job?

2. How have your job duties changed over the last three years? The last year?

3. Do you have more responsibilities than when you started?

4. Are you overloaded with work?

5. Does the nature of your job cause you to interact frequently with other departmental managers?

6. Can you see a progression from where you were three years ago to where you want to go within the company? Do you have an action plan?

7. Are you excited by what you do or a little bored?

8. Is your job fun?

If you've been doing the same job for a period of time with little reward, recognition or promotion, chances are your sense of motivation is slipping. No need to despair. The real problem might be with your company.

Look around and try to determine how your company motivates its top-level managers and supervisors. Ask yourself these questions:

1. Is the managing director a motivated, charismatic leader?

2. Does the managing director imbue projects with a sense of excitement and purpose?

3. Do the managing director's attitudes filter down the management hierarchy and inspire subordinates?

4. Does your immediate supervisor take responsibility for motivating you?

5. When you make suggestions, does your boss listen?

If your boss doesn't take an active part in helping you get promoted, recognize your achievements, or hand you a bonus for a job well done, then it's difficult for you to pass on a sense of passion and commitment to your staff.

Internal versus external motivation

Occasionally an uninspired department can pull together and accomplish miracles. It's usually a crisis situation which requires employees to pit themselves against unbeatable odds – and win. Working towards a specifically defined short-term goal in a crisis situation is considered external motivation. The results can be spectacular. Employees who formerly approached their work with a lacklustre spirit can surprise the most seasoned manager with their innovation and creativity. Likewise, a somewhat uninspired manager can be transformed into an inspired group leader by the dynamics of external motivators. As one business expert puts it, 'By nature, people are interested in doing well, in being effective workers and effective achievers'.

External motivators work because:

1. they allow group work habits to change, becoming more creative and productive;

2. they allow individuals to discover and develop their hidden talents through brainstorming, work planning, and dynamic communication;

3. the group learns to play as a team, to pull together towards a common goal and to win;

4. individuals learn to value themselves as part of a productive, innovative group;

5. when external motivators involve bonuses, incentives or recognition, individuals feel honoured and duly compensated.

Unfortunately external motivators have a limited life-span. Their effectiveness usually lasts the length of the project or however long it takes to achieve the specified goal. When the carrot is taken away, a highly motivated department can easily slip back into low productivity. External motivators work like sugar in the bloodstream. They can produce short bursts of high energy, good for achieving short-term goals but lacking the sustaining power of internal motivators for more long-term efforts.

When external motivators are based exclusively on financial rewards they can be interpreted as coercion, which breeds frustration and resentment among employees.

In the long run, internal motivators work better than external motivators because they build on a psychological structure already in place – self-esteem.

Employees need to know their company cares about them. Effective managers are able to communicate that caring, but to do so they must genuinely care about themselves. Self-esteem is the hidden ingredient in a motivated leader's formula for success.

To determine your level of self-esteem, ask yourself the following questions:

1. *Do I continually compare myself to others – and feel I don't measure up?* If so, you need to understand that everyone is different and possesses diverse talents and abilities. Learn

to value your own abilities, opportunities and achievements as unique.

2. *Do I reward myself for a job well done?* If not, get in the habit of rewarding yourself. Try dinner at a favourite restaurant or going to a movie with a friend. Also, concentrate on internal rewards; give yourself a pat on the back and bask in the glow of meeting a goal.

3. *Do I accept praise well or does it make me uncomfortable?* If you're uncomfortable, become aware of your body language. Practise looking your colleague in the eye and saying, 'Thank you. I worked hard on that project. Your appreciation means a lot to me.' Let it sink in. Hear praise while it's being given. Replay it to yourself afterwards.

4. *Do I accept what's positive about myself?* If not, get reinforcement for your positive attributes from friends and colleagues. Don't dwell on past mistakes. View problems as opportunities to learn.

5. *Do I indulge in self-criticism?* If so, reinforce your self-confidence with positive imagery and affirmations. 'I can handle this easily. Managing this project is fulfilling and fun for me.' Disconnect yourself from negative inner voices. Become your own cheerleader. Be objective. Ask yourself, 'Is this criticism

justified? Does it serve a positive purpose?'
If not, get rid of it.

Internal motivation pays off in the long run
because it's not dependent on the artificial structure
of meeting a deadline, satisfying a quota or topping
a departmental sales record. When you're motivated
from within, your employees trust you for your con-
sistency. They see that there's no slackening off as
certain goals are met – that commitment to high
quality is permanent.

Mission statements – does yours match your company's?

Your company has a mission statement. Do you? It's
important to know *why* you're working and *what*
you're trying to achieve, both on a personal and
managerial level.

A mission statement is not an action plan. Action
plans are specific steps with measurable results that
will help you achieve your predefined goal. For
instance, your five-year action plan might look
something like this:

1. Boost next year's departmental production
   by 20 per cent. Decrease turnover by 25 percent by incorporating stronger team-building.

2. Increase lateral networking. Offer my department's services to help test Research and Development's ideas. In turn, initiate brainstorming in R & D that can benefit marketing.

3. Use interdepartmental support and documentation to ask my boss for a promotion.

Mission statements are much simpler than action plans. Your company's mission statement states why and for what purpose the organization was formed – what services, goods and ideas it offers the public, and what its standards are.

Your mission statement may be short term or project related. If so, chances are you're more involved in putting out fires than in seeing the big picture. You're reacting to external stimuli rather than acting out of internal beliefs and values.

Your mission statement should reflect what you really want to do with your life. Commitment to a personal mission is the cornerstone on which high performers build their success. What is your greatest desire? What do you hope to achieve by working for the company that employs you? See if any of these answers fit you:

1. To become the first woman director.

2. To do the best job I can, to listen to my employees attentively, to let them know I care.

3. To have a hand in guiding my company's development from a small manufacturer to a multibased international corporation.

4. To grow with this company, both psychologically and technically. To meet the demands of effective managing with clarity and purpose. To develop expertise.

Write down your personal mission statement. Then assess if you can realistically achieve what you want in your current job. See if your personal mission statement and your company's mission statement are in harmony. A good blend of the two will allow you to:

1. organize your experience around a single unifying theme;

2. seek and find a purpose;

3. feel proud of yourself;

4. achieve goals;

5. make a contribution;

6. follow your action plans purposefully and tenaciously.

One common demotivator for talented managers is being stuck in the wrong company. Certain kinds of work environments and corporate policies can actually alienate enthusiastic performers. Ask yourself if your company places any of these unnecessary obstacles in your path:

1. *Citing historical precedent.* 'This is the way we have always done things in the past.' Most businesses know by now that this non-innovative attitude is the quickest way to the corporate graveyard. It favours rigidity and outmoded practices over creativity and new information.

2. *Bad supervision.* The company employs managers who give orders without explanation. They're impatient with subordinates who complain of boredom, pointless work, lack of opportunity. This attitude is adversarial and counter-productive. Instead of listening to employees and seeking ways to address their complaints, managers view employees as undermotivated and lazy. Employees, on the other hand, view their managers as callous and indifferent.

3. *Bureaucratic organizational structure.* By its very nature, bureaucracy does not foster good communication (the boss talks, the employee listens). The organization's over-involvement with red tape, meaningless details and policies frustrates any attempts to make positive changes. Employees feel they are of no consequence to managers above them in the bureaucratic hierarchy.

Your ability to make changes in the above scenarios depends on your rank and position – how much power you actually wield. Companies in trouble, with sliding sales figures and poor morale, may be willing to listen. You can introduce new management concepts based on:

1. *Participatory management.* Managers seldom make unilateral decisions, preferring to increase employee involvement in a work climate that is reward centred.

2. *Management by objectives.* Managers explain to workers the results they expect, then allow workers to decide how to achieve those ends by prioritizing tasks and measuring their own performance.

3. *Quality circles.* Workers are recognized as experts by utilizing a small group of employees in the same work area who have been trained to identify and analyse problems related to their own jobs.

Depending on your level of motivation and commitment, you can offer your own department as a pioneer group to put these management theories into practice. Do your homework, however. Before making such a proposal:

1. poll your employees to find out if they'll support your decision, and discuss

your ideas openly with those who oppose them;

2. find out how much time it will take for these management practices to get results, talk to managers in other companies who have adopted more flexible approaches, and give yourself a realistic time span in which your efforts can mature;

3. make sure your company is behind you, that you aren't being set up to fail – if necessary, get written statements of support and make sure other departments can't sabotage your work.

Even if your company decides not to adopt your management techniques, you'll have the satisfaction of developing better work relationships with your employees. If your proposal is accepted, on the other hand, you will have the external motivator of being in the company spotlight. Your employees will perform better, work harder and become better team players.

What are the characteristics of a motivated manager?

To determine how motivated you are, look at how well you motivate others. Ask yourself how well you've incorporated the following skills into your own management style:

1. *Recognize your employees' strengths and talents.* Just as no two snowflakes are alike, so no two people are alike. Different employees have different abilities. Maybe you're not aware that your rather mediocre word-processing technician has outstanding accounting abilities. Watch. Listen. Be on the lookout for talented, ambitious employees who take classes to hone their skills, who ask for additional training.

2. *Help your employees recognize and appreciate their own abilities.* Avoid letting your employees become competitive with one another, comparing skills, income, lifestyles, etc. Listen to and nurture each employee separately. Help your employees uncover and develop their special gifts.

3. *Don't ignore weaknesses.* Don't dwell on them, either. Help your employees recognize and correct their own weaknesses.

4. *Don't treat subordinates like children.* Don't manipulate employees, order them about or tell them what they must do. Motivate them to take the initiative for improving their performance. Help them understand the value of playing by the rules.

5. *Assess the best way to deal with each situation.* No two employees are alike. No two employees will react the same way to criticism, counselling or reprimands. Don't be too docile or conciliatory. When the situation demands it, take control.

6. *When correcting employees, focus on their behaviour, not on their personalities.* Never undermine an employee's ego or self-esteem. Follow the golden rule of management: when administering praise, do it publicly; when administering criticism, do it privately.

7. *When problems arise, instead of blaming, look for solutions.* Enlist employees' co-operation in problem solving. Try to depersonalize the mistakes that have caused the problem.

8. *Be honest, trustworthy and straightforward.* When you make mistakes, admit them. Trust is the foundation of team spirit. Employees need to know they can trust their bosses to deal with them honestly.

Basically, management experts say, everyone wants to do well. Workers are already motivated; managers just have to remove the obstacles.

To ensure your own peak performance, it's important to realize that high achievers are no different from you or your employees. They're not people with a mysterious 'X' factor added. They're people with very little of their potential taken away.

To be a motivated performer, do two things:

1. Develop within yourself an ability to achieve what you set out to do.

2. Cultivate within yourself the characteristics you value most.

Summary

In this chapter we've examined your level of motivation by:

● Taking a look at what motivation actually is: defining the difference between external and internal motivators. A high degree of internal motivation will take you where you want to go. Much of your motivation is based on self-esteem.

● Examining your personal mission statement and determining if you're working in the right kind of environment.

● Enumerating the characteristics of a motivating manager and how a motivating manager deals with employees.

Basically, employees need to know their managers are honest and trustworthy. Next, they need to know they care about them. That's the tough part of motivation. The rest is knowing successful techniques.

3

Ways to motivate: team building

It's an old adage that two heads are better than one for solving problems. No matter how gifted the individual player, he can accomplish a great deal more if he is part of a dedicated team.

Team building is an effective motivational device that creates a group identity. Since teamwork is an integral part of corporate life, you need to understand how it works. In this chapter we'll look at:

- why team play works in corporations;
- what team-building skills you, as a manager,

need to develop;
- how to keep your team in the game.

Why team play works in corporations

As children, nearly all of us experienced the thrill of victory, whether playing football, hockey or netball. We all remember basking in the warm glow of winning – learning to value ourselves and our teammates for the special combination of talents and abilities that made us winners. People exposed to team play in sports at an early age learn invaluable lessons that can later be applied to corporate life. They are:

1. *Know the game plan.* The goal is to win the game. A good coach has a strategy for winning. Every team is different, therefore every game that pits one team against another is different. Know your team's strengths and weaknesses. Know your opponents' strengths and weaknesses. Work out how your team can maximize its strengths against the opposition.

2. *Know the rules and play by them.* A good coach teaches a team the rules and insists they play fair. The team that doesn't abide by the rules will be penalized. A good player doesn't limit learning the rules that apply to his or

her own position only. A good player will learn the rules that govern the overall game as well as those specific to each player's position. This approach gives the team flexibility: the ability of one player to play another's position.

3. *Know your position and how to play it.* A structured, organized team functions in the same manner as any other well-defined social unit. Depending on their innate talents or experience, each player occupies a certain position on the team. With that position come certain responsibilities. A player knows how his or her duties fit into the overall operation of the team. When well motivated, he or she performs to the best of their ability, is a credit to the team and ensures its success. Personal glory and recognition are secondary to the good of the team.

4. *It takes all types to make a team.* Not all players are equally good at the same endeavours. Some are fast runners, some are strong hitters, some are great pitchers. Some teammates are good as individuals and some are bad, some are extremely capable, some have fewer skills to contribute to the team effort. Nevertheless, each member must adjust to the others and learn to play with them as a team. Divisiveness among team-mates is not allowed – it's simply bad sportsmanship.

5. *Don't question the coach's decisions.* Every team needs a leader, a decision maker, an arbiter. The coach is the ultimate authority and motivator and while team members may not always agree with the coach's decisions, they are obliged to implement them. Although all players participate in the planning sessions, the coach makes the final decision in planning strategy and dictating plays.

6. *Learn from losing.* The best games are played between two evenly matched opponents. It's no fun when teams are grossly mismatched in terms of their abilities. When both teams are playing their best, there's no dishonour in losing. Learning how to lose gracefully becomes part of the bigger game plan. If the possibility of losing didn't exist, there would be no sense in trying to win and no motivation to improve. Teams learn to take defeat in their stride. They learn to treat failure as a revitalizing force. Losing a game signals the need for more practice, better techniques and improved team co-ordination.

Basic team-building skills

Obviously, not everyone on your team of corporate players has had exposure to the concepts outlined above. You might even be feeling somewhat intimidated by your own lack of experience in unifying and motivating a diverse group of people.

It's simpler than it sounds. As a manager/coach you need to keep in mind four basic strategies that can help you incorporate team building:

1. Perceive the goal.

2. Devise a strategy so you can reach it.

3. Motivate the team to do it.

4. Prepare to overcome obstacles that stand in your way.

Goal setting is the first major element in team building. It unifies team members by giving them a shared sense of mission or objective. The second element in team building is how well you communicate that goal to your team.

To set goals effectively you must have a clear idea of what they are. Whatever the goal, make sure you share the game plan with your staff. Don't simply dictate your wishes. Make them feel their involvement is important and that they are part of the process. Show them they're critical to the project's outcome and why you're proud to have them on your team. Do this by:

1. Communicating to team members why the goal is important.

2. Showing them why their involvement is critical.

3. Showing them how they will benefit from its success.

Why the goal is important

It's hard for team members to pull together to reach a common goal unless they understand why that goal is important. Here are some strategies that can help you reiterate the importance of what your team is doing.

- *Be enthusiastic.* Share your sense of mission and enthusiasm with team members. Communicate not only your excitement, but also the significance of what the team is doing, why it matters to the company and what the outcome means for the team.

- *Be specific.* Don't generalize with comments like, 'As part of Research and Development, we're going to come up with the best ideas this company has ever had'. Instead, make your objectives concrete and achievable: 'To increase sales, this department needs to improve the product we offer our customers. Here's how we're going to structure a new pilot programme and here's the percentage of market turnaround we're aiming for.' Come to every team meeting with information that reflects the team's accomplishments. Convey a sense of activity and accomplishment through visual aids, reports and feedback from individuals to whom you've assigned duties.

● *Be informative.* Share information. Be thorough; give team members the history of the project. Tell them its background, why it's a priority, who made what decisions. Let them know what impact it will have on the company as a whole.

● *Be realistic.* To motivate effectively, the goal must be clear and attainable. If possible, state each goal in terms of what the employee must contribute instead of merely forecasting the outcome. You might achieve your best results by explaining the goal, then allowing each team member to identify their contribution within given parameters. Let each team member set specific targets.

● *Be flexible.* Realize that the goal may change as your team works through the process of achieving it. Be willing to change as the goal changes. Keep communications clear and open.

Show your team members why their involvement is critical

Team building is one of the best ways to encourage employees to motivate themselves and each other. Consistently conveying that the company cares about them is one of the most efficient ways to inspire their self-motivation. You can communicate that you and the company care by practising the following:

- *Know your players and their individual goals.* Before tackling the first big kick-off meeting, do a little investigating. Talk to each individual who will be playing on your team. Find out what motivates them. Explain how the team's success will meet each person's individual goals.

- *Include, don't exclude.* You need strong team members who feel they're a vital part of the group. When people feel important and included, you motivate them. Create a team atmosphere that welcomes outsiders, is embracing and nurturing. The motivation that stems from inclusion builds bridges between individuals and the group as a whole. Exclusion, which occurs when petty variables and negativity exist, builds walls.

- *Value the individual.* Let team members know you value each person for their individual talents and abilities. Discourage competitiveness among players. Encourage innovation and creativity by conducting brainstorming sessions where there are no wrong answers. Develop and maintain your sense of humour.

Communicate the benefits of success

Whenever possible, reiterate how team members will benefit from the project's success. Be careful how you do it. Sell, don't tell. As manager, your job is to persuade, not to order.

- *Rewards that motivate.* If a successful outcome includes a cash bonus or a Caribbean cruise, use the reward as part of your movitation strategy. Effective rewards include recognition (an awards banquet), promotions and affirmations of the individual's effort from other managers in the company.

- *Being on the team.* It's possible that some of your team members have never played on a team before – much less a winning team. Stress the benefits of teamwork. By project's end, everyone on your team will have demonstrated their ability to take on additional responsibility, meet goals and motivate one another.

- *Emphasize training.* Team members can derive benefits if they are asked to cross-train –

learn other team members' jobs. They may also be 'guinea pigs' in product research – the first to test new software or managerial methods, or sell new products. Convey to your team members that these 'firsts' put them on the cutting edge in their industry and give them a wider spectrum of skills and abilities, and thus a better chance of future promotion.

How to keep your team in the game

You've got your team assembled and everyone seems eager and willing to work together. A week later, it's a different story. Some players are apathetic, others are confused and some are downright hostile towards you and towards each other. They feel the time spent on the team is jeopardizing their 'real jobs'. What do you do?

1. *Define roles*. This should be your first step. If you already did it, then redefine roles. You may have to do this at each team meeting by asking for progress reports that are identified with team positions. Reiterate with comments like, 'Maloney, as I recall, you're in charge of our database management. Would you like to fill us in on where your retrieval system stands?'

   You can avoid power struggles by documenting each person's responsibilities and authority within the group. When there are questions, check the notes of the appropriate meeting. Follow up meetings with memos that outline decisions and action plans. Make sure each team member is on the distribution list. Ask for comments on the memos at the next meeting.

2. *Draw up a game plan.* Players need to know what's expected of them in advance. Each player must understand what they need to do and what everyone else needs to do to reach the goal. If you feel there's some confusion, ask players to reiterate their responsibilities: who they communicate with, which players they're in charge of, who they need approval from to go ahead, and so on.

3. *Create an identity for the team.* Give your team a name which makes its players proud. Call it the 'Task Force for Research and Development'. Let the team name itself. Put an item in the company newsletter that explains why the team has been created and what its goals are. Discuss the team and its mission in departmental meetings, mention players and their positions by name. Your team members will feel connected to the rest of the company as well as important and recognized. Giving your team an identity helps individual players become visible. Feeling they're in

the spotlight is an excellent way to ensure co-operativeness among team members.

4. *Be willing to reassign positions.* A good manager gives the right job to the right person at the right time. Observe your players; find out which ones are your 'people people' and which are your 'paper people'. The former are better at interacting with others, usually possessing highly developed verbal skills. The latter are your 'techies' – more interested in working with technology, concepts and ideas. 'People people' excel in the following positions: customer service, negotiation, training, presentations and supervision. Paper people are good at research and analysis, design, technical writing, operation and troubleshooting. You might want to switch a team member to another position if they are not suited to their current one.

5. *Give your players a chance to stretch their skills.* When an employee is playing his or her position too easily, you might want to switch them to a more difficult position. Use assignments as rewards for top performers and you'll get better results.

6. *Encourage networking.* Give players the freedom to stay in frequent contact and exchange information with each other. At your first meeting, establish how the team

will communicate (through correspondence, memos, bulletin boards, electronic mail, etc.) and how often. Make sure team members know how to reach each other after hours, and who has authority to make decisions when you're not available.

7. *Reinforce the team concept at every opportunity.* When the group has done well, praise the entire group. Don't praise individuals before the group. If an individual team member has performed in an outstanding manner that you want to recognize, take them aside and praise them privately.

The key to establishing and maintaining good team-work is to create a caring atmosphere. If employees believe their manager, and hence their company, truly cares about them, high performance naturally follows. To communicate this, you must demonstrate:

- a sense of excitement and commitment to the team's defined goal;

- an appreciation and support for the team as a unit and for individual team members.

Summary

In this chapter we've looked at how team work functions on the corporate level. We've examined some of the basics every team member learns as a child and applied them to the workplace.

You need to know the game plan and be able to communicate it to your team. Capitalize on team members' strengths to reach the goal. Work out the rules and how to play by them. The better your players understand the rules, the better they'll be able to cover their own and other players' positions.

One of the most important team-building skills you can have as a manager is the ability to communicate why the goal is important. You can do this by being enthusiastic, specific and informative. Show your team members why their involvement is critical. Explain to each individual how the team's success can help realize individual goals.

And finally, once your team is in the game, keep them motivated by keeping roles defined, having a clear game plan and giving the team an identity. If you run into trouble, don't be afraid to reassign positions that will give your players a chance to stretch their skills.

4

Ways to motivate: delegation

Delegation is one of the most successful means a manager has to increase teamwork. When handled properly, it's a way to improve the abilities of your employees, build their confidence and encourage them to take risks. In addition, top managers use delegation as a way to enhance their own strengths.

To delegate well, however, managers must perform a delicate balancing act – juggling their employees' needs for greater autonomy with their own needs to remain in control. Delegation is not as simple as it sounds. It can be a big demotivator when employees feel their eagerness to prove themselves has been exploited by callous management or if they equate delegation with manipulation by company bosses.

Ideally, however, delegation can be your means to hone a team of top performers. It can free you of time-consuming management details and make you a better leader.

In this chapter, we'll show you the secrets of effective delegation by examining:

- what delegation does;
- when to delegate;
- ways to delegate effectively.

What delegation does

It's the job of management to accomplish organizational goals through the efforts of others. To be effective in reaching goals, managers must have the confidence to delegate responsibility and authority to their employees. The more your staff can achieve, the more successful your entire company can be. Therefore, delegation benefits both bosses and their subordinates by:

- giving a manager more time so he can be a more effective leader;

- empowering employees by giving them greater autonomy and responsibility;

- promoting teamwork between management and workers by creating an open atmosphere of trust.

The concept of delegation is undergoing continuous change. Traditionally, it meant assigning various tasks and responsibilities to one's employees. A more enlightened approach is for management to delegate by removing obstacles so that employees are freer to do their jobs. Whatever your approach to delegation, it's important to know some basic 'Dos' and 'Don'ts'.

1. *Do* use your authority to delegate. If you don't use your authority, you lose it.

2. *Do* delegate the necessary authority when you delegate responsibility.

3. *Do* delegate only to employees who you are confident can handle the authority.

4. *Do* clearly define the responsibilities delegated to each subordinate.

5. *Do* follow up to be sure the job is getting done, but avoid 'over-supervising'.

6. *Do* back up the employee you've delegated work to with your support.

7. *Do* be clear with each subordinate what decisions he can make.

On the other hand:

1. *Don't* interfere unnecessarily with the work you've delegated.

2. *Don't* use delegation as a way to offload your duties on to subordinates. Its purpose is to provide you with an increased capacity for greater responsibility.

3. *Don't* delegate in such a way that your employee ends up with 'dual supervision' – is accountable to more than one boss.

When to delegate

Scenario A

A bright young managing director of her own athletic footwear company found that rapid growth brought as many problems as rewards. In less than two years, sales had climbed from zero to £10 million. The final battle of priorities occurred during the planning session of the annual trade show. The managing director had to make a difficult decision. Should she oversee the myriad details for the show, which was important to maintain her company's sales, or should she spend the time interviewing retailers? 'I just couldn't do everything myself. I knew that if I didn't delegate, some area in my company would suffer', she recalls. Literally forced to

delegate, the managing director chose to let her public relations manager handle the planning of the
trade show. The results? 'Orders exceeded our
expectations.'

How does this managing director feel about her
choice to delegate? 'Good. Employees need guidance and freedom to do their jobs right.'

Scenario B

The chairman of a company which provides tour
services began having trouble managing the business he founded in 1972. His current operations
employed 1,000 people, yet he was managing them
the same way he did when there were just 100
employees. 'I was functioning as a dictator,' the
president recalls. 'I was reaching the point where I
could not do everything on my own. I had to release
some of the authority and responsibility?'

Luckily, his vice-director encouraged him to
attend a series of management courses that stressed
the need for clear communication of objectives and
delegation. Taking these principles to heart, the
chairman began actively delegating responsibilities
and communicating goals and objectives to everyone in the organization. Before, he feels, the chain of
command was very unclear. It made delegation very
difficult. Now each employee is introduced to all
other facets of the business as well as organizational
charts. 'We learned that you cannot delegate successfully and expect an employee to function at his

optimum unless the manager has been successful in conveying the big picture to him.'

In both situations, knowing when to delegate was half the battle. Ideally, managers have highly motivated, talented staff members all primed and ready to jump into a demanding project designed just for them. But it seldom works that way in real life.

Unfortunately, delegation is often a panicked response to a crisis situation. The times you're most likely to delegate are in response to outside pressures. For instance:

- when an unexpected growth spurt has strained your company's resources to maximum capacity;

- when your company has developed and diversified over a period of time, yet business is still being conducted as if the company were much smaller;

- when your job, because of added responsibilities and deadlines, has become unmanageable;

- when your talented subordinates are bored and under-utilized – ripe candidates for divisiveness and political in-fighting.

Ideally, managers should delegate only to employees they have confidence in. But it's important to remember that delegation can often turn an undermotivated, troublesome employee into a high achiever and solid team player.

Good managers don't wait until a situation is beyond control to delegate. Knowing when to delegate is as important as what you delegate. Begin delegating when:

1. You or a staff member are overloaded. Delegation is not a permanent re-assignment of work and duties, but a temporary redistribution.

2. An employee would benefit from the experience of having his abilities tested by a new assignment. The delegated work could help prepare a promising employee for a future promotion by allowing him to demonstrate new skills.

3. You can monitor the outcome of the work. Never delegate when you have no means of reviewing and approving work methods and results. Should the employee be unable to handle the delegated work, have an alternative solution available.

4. It's an assignment you would like to do, but can't. Never 'dump' unwanted tasks on employees. They'll resent the assignment and you.

Ways to delegate

Delegation does not mean simply asking an employee to complete a list of tasks. The problem with that approach is that the employee is placed in a bind: he must carry out responsibilities without having the ability to make decisions on how the tasks should be done. Managers who pay lip service to delegation, but secretly hang on to control, are doing their staff a grave disservice. Delegation *without* control is a big demotivator.

Delegation means giving a subordinate enough authority to complete the task. Managers must consider their employees' individual capabilities and then provide them with whatever authority is required to fulfil the assigned responsibilities and establish an acceptable method of checking on the employee's progress. It can be viewed as a three-step process.

1.   *Assign responsibility.* When you delegate, be sure to convey responsibility. Make sure the employees understand that the task they have been assigned is important to you and that you have confidence in their ability to complete it successfully.

2.   *Provide authority and support.* Make the limits of his or her authority clear to the employee. Provide them with support by explaining their authority to their peers. Make sure they

understand they are not to abuse their authority. Remember that delegating with limited authority (your continual checking to see if everything is running smoothly) contradicts the purpose of delegation.

3. *Hold the employee responsible for the outcome.* Make it clear the delegation is a vote of confidence in your employee's ability to meet goals. Provide the employee with checkpoints at consistent, predetermined times. For instance, you can keep tabs on operations through weekly check-up meetings.

Problems in delegating

Occasionally, delegation causes rather than solves problems. Delegation involves a certain amount of risk. Good managers have carefully calculated their odds of success and failure and know what a failure will cost them. By delegating, a manager chooses to turn over work he or she knows they can do but they lack the time for, to an employee they assume can do the work. When problems arise it's because managers have misjudged the demands of the assignment or the ability of the employee. Here are some common problems and steps managers can take to avoid them:

1. The employee to whom you've delegated responsibility starts to slack off, procrasti-

nates and fails to meet deadlines. At this point you should call a meeting, define the problem and develop alternatives. Try to avoid taking the project away from the employee, if possible; but sometimes it may be your only solution.

Other options include:

● When the problem is technical, assign a staff expert to advise the employee.

● When the problem is a lack of motivation, assign a coach to the employee to give guidance through the rough spots.

2. The deadline is suddenly shortened on the project you've delegated. However, your employee requires more than the available time to finish it. In this case, get feedback from your employee. Explain how the deadline has changed. Ask for ideas on how the deadline can be met. Give them the option of sticking with the project. Offer expert help and round-the-clock guidance. Come to a solution that is mutually satisfactory so your employee doesn't feel pressured to (a) finish a highly pressured project, or (b) abandon a rewarding project midway to completion.

Finally, once you've delegated, stay out of the way.

Managers who are too controlling don't allow employees the autonomy to get involved and structure their own work. Over-controlling managers may think they're delegating, but in reality they are secretly threatened by employees being in charge of their own work. The controlling manager wants employees to do it his or her way. The outcome is a gradual slowdown of productivity and diminishing of morale.

Take it from a smart delegator who says: 'Management's job is to remove the obstacles so employees can get in there and do their jobs.'

Summary

In this chapter we've discussed delegation as an important motivational tool.

Delegation benefits both bosses and subordinates in three ways:

1. It gives managers more time to take on more leadership responsibilities.

2. It empowers subordinates.

3. It promotes teamwork between management and staff.

Delegation often occurs at the least opportune moment. But it can be used effectively to stave off crises brought about by:

1. rapid company expansion;

2. resistance of a company to management planning;

3. under-utilization of talented staff.

Good managers know it's appropriate to delegate when:

1. they're overloaded;

2. the delegated responsibility would benefit an employee;

3. they can monitor the progress of the delegated assignment.

Finally, managers should delegate authority as well as responsibility. With authority, an employee has greater autonomy over his own work. Avoid being over-controlling and offloading unwanted tasks rather than delegating important projects.

5

Ways to motivate: communication

Ask any good manager and they will probably tell you that communication skills are among the most important sources of personal power. Being able to convey the big picture to one's employees is a major motivational tool. Yet many managers do not realize that *how they communicate* is just as important as *what* they communicate.

Along with the concept of teamwork as a means of building organizational unity comes the need to communicate more effectively. Enlightened managers no longer shout orders and yell at employees who disobey them. They realize communication is a means by which they can solicit employees' opinions to shape objectives, because when it comes to being managed, employees don't resist their own ideas.

This communication technique requires well-developed listening skills. As the chairman of a successful computer manufacturing company says: 'In this organization we listen more than we talk because we think that is the best way to learn'.

In this chapter we'll look at various aspects of good communication and how it keeps your staff motivated:

- what makes people want to listen to you;
- what to communicate;
- how to communicate;
- meetings which motivate;
- how to listen well.

What makes people want to listen to you

We've all had the uncomfortable experience of being in an audience, shifting restlessly in our seats while a speaker drones away behind a podium. They might even be discussing a subject we're interested in, yet something about their manner or style of presentation is boring.

And then we've had the reverse experience.

We've listened rapt and attentive, practically on the edge of our chairs, as a speaker mesmerizes us, shares their personal experiences with us and energizes us with their magnetism and charm.

Charisma is the mysterious, unmeasurable substance that makes people recognize and follow leaders. Most successful communicators are gifted with a certain amount of charisma. With seemingly no effort they're able to draw us into their web of words and make their concerns our concerns. We want to be around people who project this kind of aura. They're magnetic, they're attractive, they're unpredictable.

Yet a charismatic leader can lose his or her appeal as easily as they acquired it. What separates leaders people want to listen to from entertaining performers is their credibility. You might have the greatest ideas in the world, but to communicate and implement them effectively you must be, above all, credible to your employees. The purpose of your communication may be to convey information, to influence and motivate others and to seek more information by getting others to talk; but unless your personal presence conveys authenticity, genuineness, honesty and straightforwardness, others may not trust you to guide them.

Your credibility is based on:

● *Track record*. Your track record sums up your past performance on the job, how long you've been with the company or in your present position, how well your projects have succeeded in the past and how well you work with your employees.

- *Enthusiasm*. Your enthusiasm for a project demonstrates to your employees your level of commitment. Genuine enthusiasm also acts as a powerful motivator to rally your staff around a challenging goal. Your enthusiasm can make a task seem fun and enjoyable even when it means hard work because enthusiasm is catching.

- *Being informed*. When you talk, know what you're talking about. Some people substitute opinions for facts while others rely on outmoded theories and ideas. Make sure that when you speak, especially formally before a group, you've gathered the latest information about your subject. Nothing discredits a speaker like outdated facts and statistics.

- *Being relevant*. Some speakers communicate facts well but never relate them to the immediate problems or concerns of the audience. If possible, raise key issues which relate to your audience. Keep your speeches succinct and on target.

- *Non-verbal cues*. Your words might be telling your staff one thing, but your non-verbal language could be telling them something else. Your credibility is reinforced by the non-verbal cues you're sending out based on good posture and grooming, the conviction of your handshake, making eye contact while you talk and maintaining an orderly, efficient desk.

If your communication is positive and upbeat, then your appearance, your mannerisms, the information you relate and your environment should send the same message. Being a credible communicator is half the battle. It ensures that when you have something to say, people will listen.

What to communicate

Nothing motivates employees as much as making them feel they are part of your company's decision-making process. Successful companies are discovering that an open environment which actively solicits employee feedback and acts on it promptly is the way to get a staff emotionally invested in a company's future and committed to their jobs.

Keep the channels of communication open throughout your department by:

1. *Sharing the big picture.* Communicate your vision to your team and reiterate it often. If employees are wrapped up in the details of a project they may lost sight of the ultimate

objective. Keep repeating the reasons you're all in this together. Give them concrete examples of the rewards: promotions, rises, company recognition, etc.

2. *Being generous with information.* Let your employees know immediately when plans change, when problems arise, or when any other changes occur that affect them or their jobs. Defuse the effect of rumours generated by crises and catastrophes by giving your staff day-by-day updates. Don't hoard information. In return, your employees will let you in on their grapevine. You'll hear the rumours before other managers do. Remember, the object isn't to encourage or participate in employee gossip but to maintain open communication.

3. *Giving praise frequently and criticism sparingly.* Make sure you give your staff plenty of positive feedback. Many workers complain they only receive feedback from bosses when there's a problem. Make sure you keep your communication with staff members deliberate. Praise in public; criticize in private. These signals are closely watched by the rest of your staff.

4. *Encouraging employee feedback.* Take time to listen to your staff. They probably possess expertise in areas you know little about. If

they have suggestions for improvements, give them a fair hearing. If you think their ideas are good, give them recognition. Actions speak louder than words. When they're on target, find a way to implement their suggestions.

How to communicate

Making the flow of communication smooth and easy depends on your verbal and visual style. Do you couch ideas in easy-to-understand metaphors and analogies? Do you flesh out a verbal presentation with visual aids? Are you careful to avoid using demotivating, over-controlling words?

Your skill in communicating with your staff has probably improved with experience. Here are some techniques that will improve your ability to communicate effectively:

1. *Use metaphors and analogies to make your point.* Be descriptive. Give your staff a word picture they can relate to. If you are encountering difficulties at the beginning of a project, you can soothe harassed workers by saying: 'Look at this as an informational wall we're trying to break through. We're hammering away every day and it seems as though we're getting nowhere. Then – *pow* – one day we break through and we're on the other side.'

2. *Use visual aids to demonstrate direction.* The more specific you can be, the better. Concrete examples transform abstract concepts into readily understandable facts and figures. If your goal is to increase your department's sales by a certain percentage by year end, put a graph on the wall in the meeting room. A picture or graph is a visual reminder of your goals. It will help guide you in making day-to-day decisions. Plot out results on a monthly basis and check the progress you've made in reaching your annual goal.

3. *Establish an open environment.* Keep office doors open and allow employees to decorate offices as they like as long as it is appropriate for a work environment. Avoid showing favouritism (giving a favoured employee a desk near a window) or reinforcing office hierarchy (by addressing clerical personnel on a first-name basis and management by surname). Put everyone on a first-name basis if appropriate.

4. *Schedule regular meetings.* Schedule departmental meetings at a regular time and place. Try not to change your routine or skip meetings. They don't have to be long – 15 minutes will do – but meetings are effective motivators. They tell your staff you're interested in giving and receiving information.

5. *Be a confidence builder, not a confidence destroyer.* Don't focus on what's wrong with an employee. If he or she needs correction, give specific guidance gracefully. Remember, that same employee may eventually play a key position on your departmental team. Their ability to perform well is undermined by your criticism. Watch how you use language to communicate:

- Keep your language supportive, not authoritative. Avoid using words with strong negative judgemental overtones: 'ought', 'should', 'can't', 'don't'. This kind of language conveys to your employees that you're more of a critical parent than a manager. When praising a staff member, be sure you are neither controlling nor manipulative. Both are tactics that will demotivate employees faster than a pink slip.

- When you are over-controlling you praise workers only for doing a job *your* way. Instead, give them more autonomy and plenty of praise when their action plan works.

- When you are manipulative you give positive feedback, then destroy its effect by tacking on a remark like, 'You're doing a good job, now don't screw it up'.

- Be positive and supportive. When deserved, acknowledge the hard work a staff member has done. 'I appreciate your carrying through on this assignment and doing it so well.'

6. *Find the positive.* When evaluating an employee's performance, begin by citing a particular skill or accomplishment, then move on to problem areas. When you conclude, again remind the employee of the positive aspects of his or her performance as well as the areas that need improvement.

7. *Vary your communication style to fit the employee.* Each employee is different. When one-on-one communication is required, be aware of how that particular employee is going to respond. Vary your communication accordingly. Ask yourself: How secure is he/she? How well does he/she respond to criticism? What words should I eliminate to avoid making him/her defensive? How can I ensure that this encounter will be productive, not demotivating?

Meetings that motivate

The regular departmental meeting is where your communication skills are most rigorously tested. Departmental meetings should achieve some or all of the following:

1. Try to address employees by name. Chat with them before and after the meeting.

2. Keep employees well informed about current or future developments.

3. Dispel rumour and speculation through clear and concise explanations. Ask employees what they've heard and what they think.

4. Enhance your employees' visibility within the department by encouraging interaction among employees during and after meetings through open discussion.

When not infused with the proper spirit of equality, caring and inclusion, your departmental meetings can degenerate into empty rituals that squelch any sharing of information. When this happens, you can bet real communication is going on somewhere else – probably behind your back.

Here's how to ensure a more participative meeting and to simultaneously keep it on track.

1. Hold the meeting at a time (prior to a coffee break or lunch) and in an environment that's conducive to communication. Keep it brief.

2. Prepare well in advance for even a short meeting. Have an agenda and know what your purpose is in scheduling this meeting. Make sure you achieve it.

3. Take notes during the meeting so you can follow up what was discussed with appropriate action plans.

4. Make sure that topics are work- or group-related. Departmental meetings are where you can introduce new employees, new managers assigned to other areas, new sales products, plans and anticipated changes.

5. Be honest and straightforward. Remember, *you're* the authority. Back up whatever you say with facts. If you don't know the answer, say so, but add, 'I can find that out for you'. If you make a promise, follow up on it.

6. Set aside time for discussion, but limit questions by requesting that they be held until you're through talking. Schedule no more than five or ten minutes for questions. Offer to answer any remaining questions after the meeting on a one-on-one basis.

7. Keep your tone positive and supportive. When problems arise, they should be presented in a manner that communicates confidence:

   ● *State the problem.* Make sure everyone has heard what's being discussed. 'Ted voiced his concern over how the recent oil embargo may affect our sales staff, particularly the people on the road.'

- *Clarify the problem.* Make sure you and your staff understand the real problem being discussed. If you have any information, share it. 'Am I correct in assuming, Chris, that accounting doesn't think it's feasible for us to maintain our sales staff while our country's oil supplies remain uncertain?'

- *Develop alternatives.* After clarifying the problem, open it up for discussion. Solicit opinions from all staff members. Just because an employee is less assertive doesn't mean his or her opinions are less valuable.

- *Keep the meeting on track.* If you feel the discussion is moving too far afield, exercise your authority as leader: 'Interesting as it may be, I really don't think a political recap of Middle East history applies to this discussion.'

- *Summarize.* When the brainstorming session has ended, summarize the suggestions made. List them all without attaching any value to them. Ask the group to choose the three strongest solutions.

- *Test staff members' commitment.* Ask staff for their approval to take the next step: present suggestions formally to board of directors, etc. If an innovative alternative has been offered, find out how much time individuals will commit towards its development: 'Carla thinks a mail order catalogue might be a viable alternative to maintaining a sales staff. Ted and Carla, how would you feel about producing a pilot catalogue? Will you take it to the next planning meeting?'

- *Make the decision for taking the next step.* After checking out departmental support, state the decision, backed up with an action plan. 'Ted and Carla, let's get together after this meeting and we'll target the ways information needs to be presented in a catalogue. Then we'll meet a week from today and see what we've got.'

Departmental meetings are ideal places for team building. They're good places to re-state goals, share your vision and give the team a collective pat on the back. Never use departmental meetings to praise or criticize individual performance.

How to listen well

According to management experts, listening to others' ideas is just as important – if not more so – as talking about your own ideas. Perhaps listening is difficult for you. You find yourself becoming restless and irritable when employees ramble on endlessly or are too shy and withdrawn to communicate clearly.

Being a good, motivating manager means you develop and ensure good communication with your employees. This means becoming a good listener. The key is developing empathy – putting yourself in the other guy's place. An employee can immediately sense when a boss has put his preconceived opinions on hold and is really paying attention. The employee then relaxes, opens up and talks.

Empathetic listening accomplishes the following:

1. Ensures an open flow of communication within your department. Employees know you will always give them a fair hearing.

2. Builds trust and teamwork. The more you listen to your employees, the more they'll listen to you.

3. Demonstrates your respect for the capabilities and potential contributions of others.

You can hone your listening skills by observing the interpersonal dynamics around you. Watch for the roles employees seem to adopt towards one another in departmental meetings. Observe relationships between people and between groups in the workplace. Learn to spot adversarial situations, misunderstandings and counterproductive competition between managers and employees.

The more insight you have into your employees, the better you'll be able to motivate them. Being an effective listener is an important way to gain this insight. Practise these empathetic listening skills:

1. *Let the other person do the talking.* This may not be easy, particularly if you and your employee aren't that well acquainted. You can stimulate discussion with remarks, like: 'Well, you've heard me talk for the last ten minutes. How about telling me how you feel?'

2. *Refrain from diagnosing, advising or interpreting.* Don't jump to conclusions and try to figure out the problem before you have all the facts. Encourage the employee to talk. You can do this with non-verbal cues like nodding your head, keeping eye contact, maintaining a pleasant expression.

3. *Occasionally ask open-ended questions.* Communication can be brought to a sudden halt if you bluntly ask a question that can be answered either 'Yes' or 'No'. Your employee starts to feel like he's being interrogated. Don't say, 'Tell me, Fred, do you like your job?' Ask instead: 'What three things about your job do you like the best?'

4. *Practise reflective listening.* Reiterate what the employee has said to demonstrate you listened. This gives the employee feedback yet allows you to avoid giving opinions and

advice. 'You're saying, Terry, that the report you submitted wasn't fairly reviewed.'

5. *Give information about the problem.* When the employee needs feedback from you, give it. 'I've been told this project is only scheduled to go until the end of the fiscal year and then you'll be working on something entirely new.'

6. *Never speculate about an employee's subconscious motives.* You're not Dr Freud, and practising amateur psychoanalysis could get you in trouble. If you're not careful, you may be projecting your own issues on to the employee. Deal with problems as the employee presents them.

7. *Provide emotional support while giving approval, correction or disapproval.* It's easy for employees to feel unappreciated. They want to know they did a good job and that you appreciate it. You can communicate appreciation even when you are correcting them: 'First of all, Kit, I just want to tell you what fun it is having you on our team. I appreciate your innovative approach and willingness to work through the planning stage with us. I think your third quarter projections are a little off, though. You might have to rework those.'

Summary

It's important to remember that keeping open communication in your department is a great motivator. It depends on your being three things:

1. *credible* – having the trust and respect of your employees.

2. *concrete* – keeping attention focused on the actual work at hand, not slipping into generalities.

3. *empathetic* – identifying with your employees, knowing what makes them tick.

The better listener you are, the better communicator you'll be. You can polish your listening skills by:

1. letting the other person do the talking;

2. refraining from diagnosing, advising or interpreting;

3. asking open-ended questions;

4. practicing reflective listening;

5. giving information about the problem when it's needed;

6. never speculating about an employee's subconscious motives;

7. providing emotional support while giving correction.

6

Ways to motivate: recognition

In a national business survey employees were asked to prioritize elements of job satisfaction. The factor that repeatedly ranked first was 'full appreciation of work'. Job security and good wages came in fourth and fifth, respectively.

Such responses make it clear that recognition is one of the most effective motivators managers can employ. It's also the least understood. Recognition is a way of rewarding employees for good work; but unlike financial rewards, it's free. Recognition and money are often combined – handing out bonuses at an awards dinner, for instance. But as most managers know, the motivation provided by cash incentives has a way of wearing off. Recognition, on the other hand, forges a bond between employer and employee based on the following basic human desires:

1. the need to interact with others in a meaningful way;

2. the need to do good work and enjoy a sense of accomplishment;

3. the need to receive recognition from a higher authority for putting forth your best effort.

Recognition is a strong motivator because it binds an individual employee to the work group and the organizational hierarchy. In this chapter we'll look at:

- how recognition differs from financial rewards;

- why recognition works;

- what kinds of recognition work;

- when recognition doesn't work.

How recognition differs from financial rewards

Money and recognition are the two most common

ways a manager can reward employees. Even in instances when a promotion doesn't involve a salary increase, it is still an effective form of recognition – conferring on the employee a new title, a new office and enhanced stature with the employee's peers.

As we discussed in Chapter 1, money incentives are often viewed as 'job satisfiers' – factors which attract job candidates to the company. The problem with job satisfiers is that they gradually become institutionalized and their uniqueness wears off. A few decades ago it was unheard of to offer employees a wide range of benefits and profit-sharing plans. Now these 'money motivators' are standard fare.

We'll discuss how money can successfully motivate employees in Chapter 7. For now, the following list shows you the common methods of reward, money and recognition, and how they differ.

1. *Financial Rewards*

   ● *Cash*

     – bonuses;
     – rises;
     – cash incentives;
     – profit sharing;
     – employee benefits.

   ● *Perks*

     – cruises (for top achievers);
     – paid vacations;

- paid parking;
- sabbatical;
- paid membership in professional organizations.

2. *Recognition Rewards*

● articles about an individual or winning team in the company newsletter;

● picture on the bulletin board of an employee shaking hands with the CEO;

● recognition at an awards banquet;

● public thanks from a higher authority at a departmental meeting;

● inclusion in a top club;

● small acts of recognition by a manager towards employee on a regular basis;

● continuous on-the-job training.

Why recognition works

It's easy for a harassed manager to overlook the consistent contributions of his or her staff. Recognition should be reserved for a major achievement; otherwise it will lose its meaning. Right?

Wrong! That major achievement might be happening right under your nose, yet you don't see it because there is no system in place to identify and reward solid, loyal performance. All too often, employees complain that their hard work, punctuality and years of service go unnoticed while the awards go to higher-ranking managers and executives. Without recognition, their own performance becomes lacklustre.

The first problem most companies need to address is how to train management to recognize employees' contributions. If you're a new manager in the department, review your staff's work history. Look for indications of company loyalty and hard work. Note employees who consistently arrive at work early or on time, who make helpful suggestions and who see projects through to completion with little supervision. Look for people who take pride in their work and demonstrate a commitment to their jobs day in and day out, not just during a crisis.

Recognition is one of the easiest ways to increase productivity because it boosts morale. To be effective, it should be accompanied by a symbol – an award which sets the employee apart from his peers. It can be as simple as a carnation or note of thanks for employees who pitched in on a project. It can be something more tangible that demonstrates the employee has been included in a club of top achievers. This can be a certificate, a trophy, a plaque or a sweatshirt (with team name or project name on it).

The only hard-and-fast rule of recognition is that it must reward real achievement – ideally, when a specific goal has been reached or when an individual employee's effort serves as a motivating example for others. If you're wondering where to begin, take a lesson in recognition from a manufacturer on the East Coast of America which started its own club to recognize employee contributions.

'The 100 Club' worked on a system of annual accrual of points. Employees earned points in the following ways:

- 25 points for a year of perfect attendance;

- 20 points for a year without formal disciplinary action;

- 15 points for working a year without a lost-time injury;

- 5 points deducted for each day or partial day of absence;

- 5 to 20 points for cost-saving or safety suggestions;

- 5 to 20 points for company-approved community service.

Employees who reached 100 points were rewarded with a jacket bearing the company logo and 'The 100 Club'. A simple act of recognition, but it worked. One of 'The 100 Club' members modelled her jacket proudly at her local bank, announcing, 'My employer gave me this for doing a good job. It's the first time in the 18 years I've been there that they've recognized the things I do every day.'

The same employee had earned over $230,000 in those 18 years with the company. To her, The 100 Club jacket was recognition for her work; the money wasn't.

Recognition works because it builds loyalty. You, as a manager, are rewarding loyalty with loyalty when you take the time to enquire about an employee's family. This simple act of recognition tells the employee you value them as an individual, not as a cog in the corporate machine, and that you understand that people are your most valuable asset.

Here are some simple acts of recognition that really get the message across:

1. Know the names of all your employees. Never stumble when introducing them to visitors.

2. If they have children, know their names and ages.

3. Acknowledge watershed events: marriages, the birth of a child, a graduation from son's or daughter's university.

4. Write thank-you notes. The impact lasts longer than a verbal thank-you. A proud employee can show it to friends and family.

5. Leave surprises on desks: carnations, cupcakes, chocolates, greeting cards.

6. When the pressure's on, pitch in. One boss

serves staff coffee and doughnuts when they've put in long, exhausting hours.

Simple acts of recognition are effective because employees see their genuineness. They don't feel manipulated by bosses, but appreciated by them. One employee described how recognition motivated her. 'I have an expectation that if I do well, good things will happen to me.'

What kind of recognition works

Depending on your position in the company, you are able to institute various types of recognition. Only if you're a director or managing director, for example, will you have the means to provide the more lucrative symbols of recognition: the hefty pay cheques and the generous expense accounts. Nevertheless, you should be aware of the different types of recognition and how they get results.

- *Position in the company*. This denotes title, power and rank. Professionals often have a strong identification with the company. Their position is tangible evidence of career achievement.

- *Luxurious offices*. Office size and location is frequently seen as a symbol of an individual's authority and position in the company.

- *Formal recognition of achievement.* This can come from a managing director, a respected mentor or from a leading expert in the individual's field. The more 'professional' the source of recognition, the more valuable it is. The recognition can be given at a small ceremony, during a staff meeting, or at an annual awards banquet.

- *Time off with pay.* This can take the form of extra personal time, sabbaticals or time off to attend professional meetings out of town.

- *Paid membership in professional societies and paid subscriptions to professional journals.* This translates as company support for staff specialists getting information from professional groups outside the company.

- *Being taken to lunch.* It's a small gesture, but it's an effective way of letting a staff member know you respect them as an individual, that they're special, that you're interested in their feedback, and you appreciate all their efforts on your behalf.

- *Immediate rewards.* When your staff has worked hard and helped you meet a tight deadline, act, don't talk. You can promise them annual bonuses, but for the present give them Friday afternoon off. You have repaid loyalty with loyalty. Taking action builds trust and credibility.

● *Day-to-day recognition.* Give loyal employees a day off or occasionally encourage them to take a long lunch. Stay in tune with their personal needs (enrolling in school, friends from out of town visiting, a relative's funeral) and reward them with a flexible work schedule.

● *Expanded visibility.* Some of your staff may be in the process of acquiring the skills or education that will increase their promotability. In the meantime, expand their visibility. Include them in meetings when it's appropriate. Make them feel important. They are.

● *Training.* You can do a lot to increase your staff's promotability by seeing that they are included in company training sessions. If your company doesn't offer training, initiate it.

● *Shared information.* You recognize your staff's importance when you share information about company changes with them. Seek their feedback. Act on their suggestions.

Rewards for clerical workers and other support staff often take the form of recognition. As outlined above, it's a powerful motivator for staff because it reinforces the mutual respect between manager and employee.

When recognition doesn't work

Ideally, recognition is a means of building trust and loyalty and ensuring better team effort by motivating employees. Recognition won't work, however, when it's not genuine – that is, when employees sense it's an alternative to giving them a well-deserved bonus or promotion. Depending on your company's reputation for fairness, recognition can be interpreted as a cheap way of buying off workers.

To keep recognition effective, make sure it fulfils the following objectives:

1. *Don't substitute recognition for financial reward.* If employees deserve a financial reward, make sure they get it.

2. *Make sure a recognition party is effective.* After enjoying a lavish dinner and awards presentation, it's not unusual for employees to complain 'The party was great considering how much it cost, and I would rather have had the money'. Keep the objectives of the recognition party in view: to raise morale, lower tension, recognize individuals or teams who have made significant contributions. Don't spend money just to impress employees.

3. *Reward what you ask for promptly.* When you've asked for extra effort, recognize and reward your staff promptly. Get in the habit of verbally

recognizing employees on a regular basis for their commitment to their jobs.

Summary

In this chapter we've examined the most powerful motivator managers can employ: recognition. It's also the least understood and most under-utilized motivational tool.

In summary, remember:

1. Recognition and financial bonuses are the two most commonly used rewards. To be most effective, they should be combined. The effect of financial rewards gradually wears off; recognition, however, builds loyalty and trust.

2. Recognition can be a simple gesture – a manager enquiring about an employee's family – or it can include symbols of achievement: a plaque, a certificate, a trophy, a team jacket.

3. Be aware of the many different ways you can recognize employees and know when to commend them appropriately and effectively.

4. Know when recognition isn't enough: when it's a substitute for deserved financial

rewards, when it is not handled appropriately or fails to meet motivational objectives, or when the reward doesn't match what was asked for.

7

Ways to motivate: money

Money can be a great motivator as well as a great demotivator. It depends on how you handle it. Promotions, bonuses and rises all tell an employee that his contribution is appreciated and has value. But as we say in the previous chapter, money works best when combined with recognition – the only motivator that gives an employee's work true meaning.

In this chapter, we'll look at the most common financial incentives – rises, bonuses and other financial rewards – when they get results and when they don't.

The power to reward is one of the five basic ways

in which bosses influence subordinates. Bosses alone can confer rises, bonuses and pats on the back. Strangely enough, these incentives don't always motivate as they're intended to. They can breed hostility, distrust and unrest. By understanding how financial incentives work, you'll exercise your power to reward more effectively.

What constitutes financial incentives?

As discussed in the previous chapter, financial incentives are either rewards that encourage employees to reach certain predetermined goals or 'job satisfiers' used to attract talented candidates to your company. Typical financial incentives are rises and bonuses. Others are classified as employee benefits. Still others fall more under the category of perks than actual money. Financial incentives can be any of the following:

1. *Rewards*

   - cash incentives;

   - profit sharing;

   - employee benefits (paid vacations, sick leave);

   - rewards for helpful suggestions;

   - employee savings/retirement plans;

- employee stock ownership plans.

2. *Perks*

- cruises;
- paid membership in professional organizations;
- paid parking;
- sabbatical leave.

Cash incentives can motivate employees to meet a difficult goal, especially when a company wants to increase sales dramatically or boost new products and services. Incentives, however, can encourage employees to compete against each other for short-term financial rewards. Company executives recommend using incentives judiciously and always accompanying them with verbal recognition so the employee's loyalty is reinforced.

Effective verbal recognition stresses the employee's achievement combined with thanks: 'This is in recognition for the long hours and hard work you spent on that project. We couldn't have met our deadline without your help.'

How to make pay rises work

What could be better than a rise, particularly when

an employee doesn't expect it? A rise should make both the manager and employee feel good about themselves. Unfortunately, it may fail to happen this way. When given the wrong way, the rise doesn't meet the employee's expectations. Its purpose backfires and the hard-working employee thinks it's a sign the company doesn't recognize their efforts. This can happen when:

- management gives the standard rise the company recommends without explaining that outstanding work on special projects is traditionally rewarded with bonuses;

- poor communication exists between management and employees during the performance evaluation. Rises traditionally reflect the information exchanged about the employee's work performance during the annual performance review;

- management's language during the meeting is defensive: 'I know it's not much, but . . .', 'I know it's not what you expected . . .';

- the employee competes with peers for rises. When employees share information about rises, it usually results in feelings of being inadequately or unfairly compensated.

Avoid problems by keeping your objectives in sight. Rises are usually given during or immediately after the annual performance evaluation. This is your chance to concentrate on your team-building skills. Give recognition with the rise, share information and ask for employee feedback during the evaluation process. That way you'll avoid hearing about employee dissatisfaction through the company grapevine. Remember to:

1. *Put the rise in perspective.* Most companies set a percentage increase each year for rises. When you're giving your employee his or her rise, share the big picture with them. Tell them their rise is consistent with the company-recommended standard. Then they'll be less disappointed if it is smaller than they hoped.

   If there's a specific reason the rise is smaller, explain it. 'Company profits were down this year, so the standard rise was lowered from 10 per cent to 7 per cent. The board thinks this will help get the company back up to speed.' Finally, if the employee has worked hard on a special project, recognize his or her effort and tell them when they can expect a bonus. Be true to your promise.

2. *Combine rises with feedback.* Make sure the rise is consistent with the expectations established in the performance evaluation. The purpose of the rise is to make the employee feel good about his or her job. Even a rise of

4 or 5 per cent, if handled the right way, can be viewed as an expression of appreciation.

Some bosses receive a chunk of money to be divided among their employees as rises. They decide how the money is distributed, tying merit rises to meeting performance goals. For top achievers, give plenty of recognition. 'You've done such a terrific job this year, we're giving you more than the standard rise.' Nothing motivates a top performer to keep going like recognition and reward.

Let under-achievers know why they're getting less. Be positive and constructive. This can give them the motivation to turn their work around. Make sure there are no surprises. This information should follow a detailed performance review and running dialogue about the employee's work. Set clear objectives about what the employee must do to earn a better rise in the future.

3. *Watch your language.* It's difficult not to become defensive, particularly if an employee is angry or upset about their rise. Keep cool. Explain the circumstances, don't apologize. Be empathetic, use active listening when the discussion becomes a debate. State your understanding of the employee's emotions, then restate your position: 'I understand your disappointment over an 8 per cent

rise when you were expecting 10 per cent. As I said, the company is restructuring right now. Hopefully, we can repay your loyalty and hard work more generously next year.'

4. *Match rises to performance.* You can discourage, but not prevent, employees from sharing information about rises. When employees become envious or dissatisfied, explain that their rise was tied to their job performance. Motivate them to improve their performance in the coming year by recognizing what they do well. Give them objectives to work towards.

How to make bonuses work

Traditionally, bonuses have been used to reward high-level executives, sales staff and other employees whose contributions directly affect the company's bottom line.

Yet today's managers recognize bonuses as an effective way to reward team effort and to motivate less visible staff members. Here are some essential 'dos' and don'ts' regarding bonuses:

1. *Never make bonuses automatic.* Bonuses lose their value it they're given out so routinely employees come to expect them. They are rewards only for outstanding effort.

2. *Make bonuses timely.* Give bonuses when they are deserved and as close to the results you are rewarding as possible. A bonus given six months after completion of a project loses its motivational power.

3. *Reward team effort with bonuses.* When the goals have been met by team effort, reward the team as a whole. Give equal bonuses to each team member.

4. *Lighten an oppressive workload with bonuses.* The head of an American publishing company hands out cash on the spot to boost his employees' morale during busy periods. 'When we're working on a monstrous project or we have a crazy schedule, bonuses lighten the tension in the air.'

When incentives don't work

Some companies are totally opposed to cash incentives. They claim that quality is sacrificed to quantity, and that employees end up competing against one another rather than working as a team. Cash incentives, however, aren't intrinsically good or bad. They're motivational tools. Enlightened managerial philosophy, or lack of it, determines their effectiveness.

Take it from a managing director who started his own overnight delivery service. During its first six years the company grew 8,100 per cent. By 1988 it had £12 million in sales while the rest of the industry had shrunk by two-thirds. How did this monumental growth occur? By a highly structured system of incentives.

Yet by the end of 1988, the managing director found himself surrounded by distrustful managers, dissatisfied dock workers and an unhappy sales staff. His thirst for growth had pushed employees to get their bonuses any way they could – even if it meant falsifying delivery and dock-loading receipts. As one manager noted, the only teamwork appeared on a poster in the break room. 'There was no common thread. Everyone was motivated by their own incentives.'

The managing director responded by abolishing the intricate sales incentive structure. He decided to start from scratch and organize his top people as a team. They began by writing a statement of corporate purpose. 'The process forced us to think through our priorities,' stated the managing director. The new mission statement concentrated on providing employees with an environment that 'promotes joy at work and achievement of personal goals'.

When incentives don't work, it's usually because employees feel their employer is using them. Bosses appear to be master manipulators who view employees as a means to achieve certain ends. Used this way, incentives destroy team unity and company loyalty because they act as bribes for good performance rather than as motivators.

Employees react by:

- rebelling and cheating the system;
- leaving the company;
- refusing to make the extra effort.

Incentives work as long as they don't take the place of traditional motivators: team building, recognition and broader rewards. If your company requires immense dedication from employees, use cash incentives sparingly over the short term and always combine them with recognition.

Alternative financial rewards

Innovative companies are finding ways to make money work for them. Not by spending it *on* employees, but by investing it *in* their employees.

Take Johnsonville Foods, a US speciality-foods and sausage-making company. Instead of a personnel department, Johnsonville has a Personal Development Lifelong Learning Department. Here employees meet with counsellors who help them articulate goals and dreams. They can be as varied as learning to grow roses or putting a child through college.

Each employee then receives an annual allowance to spend on a personal growth project. Some join cooking classes. Others use the money to help meet big expenses like education.

It's hardly surprising that Johnsonville experiences little turnover and its sales have risen a steady 15 per cent annually. 'We view people as an appreciating asset', says one vice-president. The rewards system Johnsonville uses doesn't run the risk of alienating employees because:

1. the rewards stress personal growth and development rather than competition;

2. the rewards motivate because they're part of a bigger management philosophy that values and recognizes employees;

3. the rewards are uniform – everyone gets the same amount, and employees can use the money any way they like;

4. the rewards are non-manipulative – employees don't feel pressured by the company to work harder to meet company goals that negate their personal goals;

5. company goals and employee goals are in harmony; therefore rewards act as fulfilments, not bribes.

Businesses have a lot to learn from companies like Johnsonville Foods. Money talks, but to act as a true reward it also has to nurture employees.

Summary

In this chapter we've discussed when financial rewards work and when they don't.

1. Rises work when:

    -   the standard company rise is explained to the employee;

    -   information about the company's financial picture is shared;

    -   they are fair and consistent with the performance evaluation.

2. Bonuses work when:

    -   they're not automatic;

    -   they're timely;

    -   they stress personal growth and development;

    -   they reward a specific project;

    -   they are given as motivators to help employees get through a work crunch.

3. Incentives work when:

    -   they're short term;

- they're non-manipulative;
- quantity doesn't threaten quality.

8

Motivational problems: the new recruit

As a manager, you know that the road to hiring the right people is never smooth and straight. First, you have to find qualified candidates. In some instances that means combing the leading business schools and colleges. Depending on your recruiting budget, you might spend days or even weeks in discussion with them, entertaining them and showing them what your company has to offer. Then, after lengthy negotiations, you make an offer. And they accept.

But your managerial job has only begun. Too

often, new recruits, full of enthusiasm and efferves-
cence, show up for work ready to take on the world.
Instead, they're shown their desk and told to tackle
a mindless task. After a month or so your new
recruit is looking distracted and vaguely dissatisfied. After six months, he's gone and the whole
process starts again.

It's something you can't afford to repeat too often.
Because if hiring an employee is expensive, losing
one costs you double.

Consider the expenses involved in filling a staff
support position:

- advertising;

- staff time spent in interviewing;

- staff time spent in reference checking and
  evaluating;

- staff time spent in filling out tax and
  National Insurance forms;

- orientation and training.

And as you know, the cost of filling higher-level
positions is much greater – sometimes amounting to
thousands of pounds to hire and train a professional employee.

A quick look at the bottom line will tell you that
it's in your company's interest to keep newly hired
people motivated. Yet few companies realize that
the first few days on the job – even the first few

hours – mould the new recruit's attitude to his employer for years to come.

In this chapter we'll look at the critical stages of a new employee's introduction to the workplace and how you and your company can make it better. We'll examine:

- the job interview;

- the first day;

- on-the-job training;

- frequent performance appraisals.

The job interview

It's natural for potential employees to be anxious to make a good impression during a job interview. But it's also your chance, as their prospective manager, to make a lasting impression on them. Research shows that employees often leave a company in a year or two unless they've been thoroughly prepared for what the job, and the company, requires. Here are some ways you can turn the job interview into a challenge that motivates qualified candidates:

1. *Be upbeat and professional in your demeanour and appearance.* Make a good impression and it will reflect well on your company. Don't resort to cynicism or making jokes about the

company. New job candidates want to work for someone they like and respect and who is enthusiastic about their job and employer.

2. *Describe the company's history and philosophy.* This is your chance to sell the company you work for to the candidate. Tell them why you're proud to be part of this outfit. Share the company vision. Fill them in on:

●   outstanding company achievements;

●   the financial health of the company – provide a copy of the annual report, etc.;

●   where the company is heading – what new markets you'll be exploring in the next decade, how the company business is diversifying or consolidating;

●   how the company reflects the innovative leadership of its owners and what part they've had in shaping company philosophy – if there's something about the company that excites you and makes you proud, say so. 'We want to avoid employee burnout. We introduced flexi-time; now we have job sharing. We're instituting sabbatical leaves for employees who've been with us a minimum of five years.'

3. *Be honest about the job requirements.* Make sure the prospective employee is given correct information regarding the duties and bene-

fits of the position. Let them know what to expect. Be specific. If it means three nights travel a week, say so. Don't make impossible promises you can't fulfil.

4. *Communicate clearly what you're looking for in a candidate.* Maybe you need people who are innovative and creative, or perhaps you value organization and loyalty. Tell your candidate about your personal values, what you think makes a good employee. That way, there will be no surprises the first day on the job.

5. *Get the candidate's feedback.* Don't get so carried away with your speech that you don't allow the candidate to interrupt, ask questions or comment freely. You may have missed or glossed over some important points. The more give and take between the two of you, the better you'll know your prospective employee when the interview is over. Ask the candidate what they're looking for in a job, in a company.

This is your chance to impress the job candidate with your company's professionalism, friendliness and efficiency.

The first day

The first day on a job is like the first day at an

unfamiliar school. You're the new kid. Everyone else appears to know their jobs and each other. It's an uncomfortable feeling for new recruits.

The first day on the job is of crucial importance, not only in making new employees feel at home, but in helping them make necessary connections with key employees and telling them their specific duties. One businessman estimated that he had worked in nearly 20 firms, corporations and institutions; none had ever spent more than a few hours in preparing him for his position in the organization.

To avoid causing your new employee to think twice about the position he or she has accepted, make sure the following bases are covered:

1. *The personnel department.* Minimize the amount of time a new employee has to spend parked in the personnel department. If it's imperative for forms to be signed, arrange for it to be done in your office or at the employee's desk. Make sure the paperwork is handled deftly and graciously. Too often new recruits lose their motivation when they are left in personnel for much of the first day.

2. *The new recruit's desk/office.* Be sure he or she knows where to hang up coats and hats and how to unlock their desk. Show them their phone and the employee phone list. But, once again, don't just leave the new recruit

there. Keep him or her motivated by keeping them in motion.

3. *Assign a guide.* Assign someone to guide your new employee through the first day. This person can introduce the newcomer to their peers and key people they'll need to know: the managing director, department heads, other managers. Show him or her where the amenities are: cloakrooms, cafeteria, lifts. Introduce the new employee to the recep- tionist to ensure that he or she will be recog- nized as an official staff member. Make a per- sonal effort to see that they get settled in.

4. *Lunch.* Take your new member of staff to lunch. Let them relax while you do the talk- ing. Share with them the general game plan for the next few weeks. Tell them about ori- entation and/or training programmes they'll be attending. Give them a sense of direction and purpose. Give them support and encouragement.

Ideally, after the first day, your new employee, motivated by a sense of inclusion, will approach job responsibilities with enthusiasm. It is crucial, how- ever, that from day one new recruits feel they're part of the team effort to reach the firm's goals.

On-the-job training

Training can consist of anything from slowly building knowledge and expertise to highly structured training lasting anywhere from six months to a year. The purpose of training is to not only acquaint the employee with their job responsibilities but also to teach:

- company policies and procedures;

- company expectations (dress code, ethics code, etc.) and culture;

- safety procedures.

Managers need to be aware that it takes time for an employee to learn a job. Allow extra time in training to master a learning curve that can involve mistakes and adjustments. A manager's responsibilities to a new employee are twofold:

1. to reach the specifics of the new job;

2. to acquaint the new employee with the corporate culture.

Companies disagree about what constitutes effective training and/or orientation. The purpose is to keep the new recruits' motivation high while building their knowledge and job skills. Two methods of training that make employees comfortable and productive at a new job are:

1. mentoring;
2. cross-training.

Mentoring

In some companies new recruits are paired with a senior executive who acts as a trainer. Mentors not only ensure that employees get day-to-day guidance and information, they also exert a socializing influence, making sure the new recruit meets like-minded employees. One advertising agency assigns two mentors to every new professional.

1. *The senior mentor.* This trainer is usually at least seven years along in their career. They give the new recruit advice and shows how the job is done.

2. *The junior mentor.* This mentor is closer to the employee's age and status and has usually had just one or two years of training. He or she is assigned to provide encouragement, support and identity, and also to act as a social connection.

When assigning mentors, managers should be careful to select employees who possess not only solid on-the-job experience but also cheerful, outgoing dispositions. The mentors should be true believers in the system – willing and ready to volunteer their time and advice. The wrong mentor can act as a big demotivator to a new recruit.

Cross-training

At a well-run manufacturing company in America, newly hired managers roll up their sleeves and go to welding school for ten months. The idea is to cross-train the people who will be in powerful positions in every area of the welding business. Company owners believe the payoff is company executives who make responsible decisions based on a wide range of experiences. The training continues for a year with employees receiving instruction in communication and other managerial arts from practitioners within the company. Steeping such recruits in the manufacturing as well as corporate culture has paid off. The people making the decisions in the executive boardroom are more informed, more sympathetic to the manufacturing side of the business and tend to see issues in the round rather than from a purely financial angle.

Frequent performance appraisals

Being interactive is a good way to keep new recruits motivated. According to one business insider, 'If you don't pay attention to them, you lose them very easily'.

Make sure the new employee is getting the feed-back he or she needs through frequent performance appraisals: quarterly is not too often during the first one or two years on the job. Ease performance fears by explaining it's your way of making sure they stay happy and excel at their job. Here are some guide-lines to follow:

1. *Applaud what they're doing right.* Give plenty of positive feedback; the new recruit is learn-ing a whole new culture. 'You've caught on quickly to these marketing research tech-niques. I'm very pleased with your progress.'

2. *Coach them on what they're doing wrong.* Give emotional support while correcting them. 'We handle this procedure a little differently. I realize it's complicated, so Sally here will take you through it a couple more times. Please go to her with any questions you have.'

3. *Ask for feedback.* Show that you are eager to learn from your new recruit as well as teach them. 'I've got some time on Wednesday and I'd like you to tell me about how you struc-tured that statistical survey. It sounds intriguing. I'm sure you've got questions, so be sure to ask me anything you don't under-stand.'

Summary

Remember that once you've gone to all the trouble to get a new employee, it's in your best interest to keep them. Here are the key ways in which you can be most effective in motivating the new recruit:

1. During the job interview:

   - be upbeat and professional;

   - fill them in on the company history;

   - be honest about the job requirements;

   - tell them what you're looking for in an employee;

   - ask them what they're looking for.

2. During the first day:

   - involve them in office life immediately;

   - show them their desk, their office;

   - assign a guide;

   - introduce them to your department, your staff;

   - take them to lunch.

3. On-the-job training:

- provide them with mentors;
- provide them with cross-training, if available.

4. During the first year, offer frequent performance appraisals:

- applaud what they're doing right;
- coach them on what they're doing wrong;
- ask them for – and listen to – feedback.

9

Motivational problems: employee burnout

It's considered normal for employees who are enthusiastic and highly motivated when they start new jobs to lose some of their momentum as the years go by. According to a recent survey, 43 per cent of first-year employees said they were highly committed to their jobs. That percentage dropped to 34 per cent for employees who had been in the same job four years or more.

Although a certain amount of employee burnout may be normal, a serious slowdown in commitment and dedication could ultimately cost a company its competitive edge. As a manager, you're responsible for creating a climate that's conducive to motivation

– not a problem when there's a new project to tackle or when your people are eager and willing to show their stuff. The issue becomes more complicated when you are dealing with employees who outrank you in seniority or have been numbed by routine, or when you're trying to stabilize turnover among minimum-wage workers.

Dealing with employee burnout requires special managerial skills. In this chapter we'll explore:

- how to recognize employee burnout;

- how to motivate long-term employees;

- how to motivate low-wage employees.

How to recognize employee burnout

Maybe you've rationalized your department's low productivity as a temporary slump, and maybe you're right. However, to find out if your sagging profitability has something to do with employees feeling derailed and undermotivated, ask yourself:

1. Are they going about their tasks with noticeable lack of enthusiasm?

2. Are my employees easily distracted from their work? Are they:

   - spending time on personal phone calls;

- taking long lunches;

- making inter-office social visits;

- not meeting deadlines;

- not setting goals?

3. In conversation, are they dwelling on off-the-job problems such as:

  - family matters;

  - conflicting priorities;

  - health problems.

4. When I correct them are they hostile and quick to anger? Are they:

  - likely to take criticism personally;

  - rebellious and political?

5. Are some employees becoming more private and withdrawn? Are they:

  - less alert;

  - absent-minded;

  - tense and irritable when they're encouraged to communicate?

Possibly the biggest cause of demotivation in an

employee is a feeling of being trapped – that their career is going nowhere. Lack of autonomy or control over one's working conditions is a big demotivator and more common among low-wage workers than higher-ranking executives.

It could be that a member of your team is badly in need of a heart-to-heart talk with the coach to revitalize their energies.

Here's what you can do:

1. *Be a good listener.* When there's a specific problem (low sales figures, little productivity) invite employees to talk about it. Try not to criticize. Listen empathetically. You might get some vital information that will help you solve a problem and better understand an employee.

2. *Be a good coach.* Give the employee feedback. Let them know the company cares about them, that they're critical to the team effort to meet goals. Compliment them on something they do well.

3. *Make work fun.* Researchers are finding that having fun at work increases productivity. Encourage the employee to approach problems as games – he or she will come up with better solutions than people who approach problems as work. Workers who report having fun at work are:

   ● absent or late to work less often;

   ● meeting work demands more effectively;

- more creative at problem solving;

- less depressed and more satisfied with their lives in general.

How to motivate long-term employees

Any manager will tell you that the more years people spend in the same job, the more you need to reinforce to them that they're important to the company.

It's not unusual for long-term employees to outrank their managers in number of years with the company. Yet, despite their experience, they may suffer from low self-esteem if they have little control over their working lives. A smart manager can counteract lack of motivation by judicious distribution of recognition and rewards. Take a look at your long-term employee and ask yourself:

1. how many years has he or she been in this present job;

2. how large a salary increase has he or she received over those years;

3. how many people report to this employee;

4. has his or her work responsibilities increased;

5. has he or she been given significant workload expansion;

6. how much departmental contact does he or she have with peers and with higher-ups;

7. does he or she receive recognition and rewards for their work, and with what frequency?

Let your long-term employee know how much the company, and especially you, appreciate them. Maybe you don't have the money in your budget to give them a badly needed bonus or payroll boost, but here are some facts of managerial recognition that get the message across:

1. Broaden their planning responsibility. Let your employee set his or her own standards and objectives. If they have subordinates, delegate more control to your employee.

2. Get them involved in departmental problem solving. Team meetings are a good way to start. If they have an area of expertise, use that as the basis for their inclusion. Ask for their contributions in brainstorming sessions.

3. Broaden their learning base. If your employee is a clerk, train him or her to do part of the buyer's duties; if they're a section head, give them some management tasks. Cross-train them in other areas within the company that complement his or her basic expertise.

4. When they contribute ideas and opinions,

reward them with recognition. Get his or her name in the company newsletter; put their suggestion, along with others, in a memo on the company bulletin board.

5. Increase their contacts with peers and other bosses in the company. Allow them the freedom to laterally network with other departments.

6. Allow them time and space to develop innovative thinking. If it looks like your long-term employee is achieving outstanding productivity, don't load them down with trivial paperwork. Give them some room to develop action plans and goal-setting procedures. Support them in company meetings when they makes contributions.

Recently, IBM had to decide what to do with long-term employees it no longer had jobs for in manufacturing, development and administration. Rather than making them redundant or giving them an extended leave without pay, IBM solved its problem in an innovative manner that benefited both the company and its employees: it put them where they were needed – a move IBM called 'redeployment'. Despite their incompatible backgrounds, the company shifted 21,500 employees into marketing and programming and another 11,800 into sales.

The results? Cross-training paid off. According to one IBM executive, 'the redeployed people were just as successful in the field as new recruits, if not more so'.

Despite dire predictions, long-term 'techies' took to sales like ducks to water. IBM recently instituted the 100 Percent Club for salespeople who achieved their quotas and proudly announced that 70 per cent of the sales team were club members. The lesson IBM has to teach managers is to stretch jobs for long-termers to offer variety and growth. Any job becomes stale after a few years. When the thrill wears off, motivation lags. Managers can avoid this by:

- Creating opportunities for the long-term employee to learn new skills.

- Shifting assignments and responsibilities.

How to motivate low-wage employees

Your low-wage employees are your company's foot soldiers. Just as an army couldn't win a battle without its infantry, your minimum-wage workers are in the trenches, dealing with customer complaints, soothing irate buyers and smiling courteously when a disgruntled customer demands their name and says, 'I want to talk to your supervisor'.

How does a manager compensate low-wage workers for their loyalty? How does a manager recognize them effectively when keeping them motivated is difficult?

Low-wage jobs are generally perceived as dead-end jobs. They require long hours of monotonous work with few or no inherent job satisfiers. Not only is the money lacking, so are traditional perks and lush benefits. Few people admire or respect low-wage workers. All these factors add up to make your job as a motivating manager of low-wage workers even more challenging.

Showing your employees you like and respect them does a lot to overcome built-in demotivators. You can make your employees feel that they're special by instilling an *esprit de corps* that gives them an identity and makes them proud to be on a team. Do this by:

1. *Making work a fun place to be.* Keep productivity and spirits high by encouraging self-expression and creativity. Encourage employees to put out their own newsletter, adopt a community charity, play in a company sports team, etc.

2. *Establishing recognition awards for the most motivated employee of the month.* Post the employee's picture where customers can see it. If they've won the award for two or more months in a row, make the award special.

3. *Cross-training employees.* Help workers overcome monotony by training them at other jobs and rotating them regularly – even within a single shift.

4. *Organizing team-building events after work.*
    Send your employees to motivational semi-
    nars, plan an annual awards banquet or pic-
    nic. Make the event one that both rewards
    and challenges them.

5. *Set up a scholarship fund.* Through raffles,
    donations or matching funds from the com-
    pany, reward outstanding employees who
    are attending college part-time with a schol-
    arship. Communicate to your employees
    that the job is a means for them to meet per-
    sonal goals.

6. *Listen and give positive feedback.* Be there when
    they need someone to talk to; otherwise,
    they'll voice their discontent elsewhere.

Ask yourself, 'What can I do to make these people
like themselves better in their jobs?' The answer lies
in teaching them to respect their jobs by working for
a manager who respects them. During team meetings, include your workers in bottom-line statistics.
Show them how much they've contributed to overall productivity. Ask them to develop their own
action plans for increasing revenues.

Don't forget to use humour when it's positively
directed: incorporate jokes, laughter, even employee-
generated cartoons. Humour shared within a group
tends to defuse tension, make meetings more productive and heighten individual creativity.

You know about the part of your employees' jobs

you can't change – the part that burns them out. Concentrate on what you *can* do to make their jobs better, more fun and more rewarding. Workers who enjoy their jobs suffer less boredom and conflict and, therefore, perform better than workers who hate their jobs.

Summary

In this chapter we've explored two common problems managers face: motivating the long-term employee and motivating the low-wage employee.

Managers should be aware of the general signs and symptoms of employee burnout. When they occur in long-term employees, managers should:

1. broaden the employee's planning responsibility;

2. involve the employee in departmental problem solving;

3. broaden the employee's learning base through training.

4. reward the employee's contribution with recognition;

5. increase their contact with peers and higher-ups;

6. give them space and time to develop innovative ideas.

Your biggest motivator for low-wage employees is to communicate your respect for them as individuals. You can do this by being creative about the way you reward your workers and making their working environment as stimulating and non-stressful as possible.

10

Six ways to motivate your employees

A manager's job of motivating employees is never done. That's because motivation takes place on a day-to-day basis. Employees watch their bosses carefully. Ideally, they'd like their managers to be role models, educators, understanding friends and visionary leaders. The best way to motivate your employees is by communicating your respect for them as individuals and providing a caring environment in which they can work. Here are the six best ways to motivate your employees.

1. *Provide leadership*. You can't motivate by words which lack conviction or isolated

actions which lack follow-through. Each day you walk into the office you demonstrate anew your purpose, your conviction and your commitment to be the best. Employees can tell when you're spinning them a line and when you live, breathe and believe what you say. Make your behaviour consistent with what you tell employees. Learn to discern the difference between external motivators (financial incentives, rewards for working toward a short-term goal) and internal motivators (words and recognition that build self-esteem). When you're internally motivated, your employees trust you to be consistent, fair-minded and true to your system of values.

2. *Team-building.* Good coaches build strong teams. Playing on a team teaches employees how to sublimate individual rewards for the good of the group. It also gives them the experience of learning to play by the rules and perform well in a position that capitalizes on their strengths. They learn to win with modesty and lose with grace. A good coach sets goals, communicates strategy clearly and creates a strong team identity. Managers motivate employees by recognizing their individual talents and making them a vital part of the overall team effort.

3. *Delegation.* To delegate well, managers must

know not only when to delegate, but what to delegate. Some managers wait until they've reached the breaking-point to hand over work to an employee. Do it before your workload buries you and before your talented employees become bored.

Nothing motivates good employees like delegation. They feel respected, included and trusted to perform well. Delegate in a timely, efficient manner that allows you time to communicate what you need to your employee and monitor the results.

Never 'offload' unwanted work and call it delegation. Delegate tasks that will stretch your employee's abilities and hone their promotable skills. Always delegate the authority needed to complete the delegated task. Give your employee your full backing and support.

4. *Communication.* If your communication is to motivate your employees, you must be credible. This means having a good track record, presenting a visual image that's congruent with your spoken message, and being enthusiastic. One way to motivate employees effectively is to be generous with information. Never hoard it. Give them plenty of feedback on company decisions and changes in directions – how overall priorities have changed. When correcting employees, be

sure you give emotional support simultaneously. Communicate in a manner which stresses appreciation for your employees' positive contributions. Avoid too much criticism; it's a big demotivator.

5. *Recognition.* Recognition is the most potent kind of reward because it stimulates an internal motivator – your employee's self-esteem. Recognition can take many forms: a picture of your employee shaking hands with the managing director; remembering to enquire about an employee's family; rewarding a hard-working employee with simple gifts and thank-you notes for a job well done. Recognition communicates appreciation from an employee's company and manager. It builds loyalty because it honours employees as a company's most valuable asset.

6. *Financial incentives.* When used sparingly, financial incentives such as bonuses can help a company reach short-term goals by boosting productivity. Financial incentives are no replacement for internal motivators, and employees should not become dependent on bonuses to work their hardest. When cash incentives are the favourite method of reward, quality is often sacrificed for quantity; team spirit gives way to individual competitiveness. Make rises work for you as a motivator, not against you. Always accom-

pany financial incentives with personal recognition, whether words of appreciation or awards banquets.

Showing your employees you respect them, that their company cares about them, is the biggest motivator of all. One way companies do this is by becoming 'family friendly', responding to employees' needs for greater flexibility in arranging their work day to help them run their families.

Surprisingly, the amount of pleasure your workers derive from their jobs doesn't depend so much on the job, its pay structure or the length of time they've done it. It depends on how much you, their manager, can communicate a sense of respect and commitment by making their jobs fun, invigorating, varied and, therefore, motivating experiences.

Index

A Systematic Approach to
Getting Results

Surya Lovejoy

Every manager has to produce results. But almost nobody is trained in the business of doing so. This book is a practical handbook for making things happen. And whether the thing in question is a conference, an office relocation or a sales target, the principles are the same: you need a systematic approach for working out:

- exactly what has to happen
- when everything has to happen
- how you will ensure that it happens
- what could go wrong
- what will happen when something does go wrong
- how you will remain sane during the process.

This book won't turn you into an expert on critical path analysis or prepare you for the job of running the World Bank. What it will do is to give you the tools you need to produce results smoothly, effectively, reliably and without losing your mind on the way.

Gower

The Motivation Manual

Gisela Hagemann

Improved productivity, flexible work practices, low rates of absenteeism,
commitment to quality, ever-higher standards of customer service - these
are the benefits of a well-motivated workforce. In this prize-winning book
the author takes modern motivational theory and shows how any
manager can apply it to create shared vision, develop mutual trust and
involve employees in the decision-making process.

The text is enlivened throughout by examples with which managers will
identify and there is a unique final section containing twenty seven
exercises designed to strengthen interpersonal skills and improve
creativity.

Gower